Look down upon me, good and gentle Jesus, while I kneel and ask you to fill my heart with faith, hope, charity and true sorrow for my sins. Help me never to sin again.

I think of your five wounds with great love and pity as I repeat the words of your prophet, David, "They have pierced my hands and my feet; they have injured all my bones."

(Say one Our Father, Hail Mary, and Glory Be, for the Pope.)

" *I* will be with you all *D*ays,

....
received

The Body of Christ for the First Time

on..

at..

....
Pastor

Even until the End of time. "

May the Blessed Mother keep under her special care the boys and the girls who learn to love her Son better by using this Mass Book.

marian
CHILDREN'S MASS BOOK

Written By
Sister Mary Theola, s.s.n.d.

Edited By
Rev. Victor Hoagland, C.P.

Illustrated By
George Angelini

Regina Press
New York

Dedication

First published in 1952, the Marian Children's Mass Book is one of the most popular Communion books ever published. Over the years it has been translated into 14 languages. This, the newly revised fifth edition, is dedicated to Charles, Edmond and George Malhame, our Grandfather, Father and Uncle, whose contributions were instrumental in its success.

George and Robert

Nihil Obstat: Rev. Francis J. Schneider
                  Censor Librorum
                  December 5, 1997

Imprimatur: Most Reverend
                 John R. McGann, D.D.
                 Bishop of Rockville Centre
                 December 10, 1997

English translation approved by the National Conference of Catholic Bishops and confirmed by the Apostolic See. Published by authority of the Bishops' Committee on the Liturgy

Copyright© 1997, 2001 by the Regina Press. All rights reserved. No part of this book may be reproduced in any form without permission in writing from the publisher.

CONTENTS

Holy Mass	11
The Church Year	52
Favorite Gospel Stories	53
Reconciliation	86
Stations of the Cross	91
The Rosary	100
The Sacraments	102
The Ten Commandments	105
The Precepts of the Church	106
Memory Prayers	107
A Visit to Church	115
My Own Prayers	120
Personal Record	122
Family Record	123
Prayer Before a Crucifix	125

INTRODUCTORY RITES

Priest: **In the name of the Father, and of the Son, and of the Holy Spirit.**
People: **Amen.**

Greeting
Priest: **The grace of our Lord Jesus Christ and the love of God and the fellowship of the Holy Spirit be with you all.**
People: **And also with you.**
(or)
Priest: **The grace and peace of God our Father and the Lord Jesus Christ be with you.**
People: **Blessed be God, the Father of our Lord Jesus Christ.**
(or) **And also with you.**
(or)
Priest: **The Lord be with you.**
People: **And also with you.**

Penitential Rite

After the introduction to the day's Mass, the priest invites the people to recall their sins and to repent of them in silence. Then one of the following forms is used.

Priest and people:

**I confess to almighty God,
and to you, my brothers and
 sisters,
that I have sinned through my
 own fault**

(They strike their breast:)

**in my thoughts and in my words,
in what I have done,
and in what I have failed to do;
and I ask blessed Mary, ever
 virgin,
all the angels and saints,
and you, my brothers and sisters,
to pray for me to the Lord our
 God.**

(or)

Priest: **Lord, we have sinned against you: Lord, have mercy.**
People: **Lord have mercy.**

Priest: **Lord, show us your mercy and love.**
People: **And grant us your salvation.**

(or)

Priest *(or other minister)*:
You were sent to heal the contrite: Lord, have mercy.
People: **Lord, have mercy.**
Priest *(or other minister)*:
You came to call sinners: Christ, have mercy.
People: **Christ, have mercy.**
Priest *(or other minister)*:
You plead for us at the right hand of the Father: Lord, have mercy.
People: **Lord have mercy.**

At the end of each of above forms is said:
Priest: **May almighty God have mercy on us, forgive us our sins, and bring us to everlasting life.**

People: **Amen.**

Kyrie
Unless included in the penitential rite, the Kyrie is sung or said by all, with alternating parts for the choir or cantor and for the people:

V. **Lord, have mercy.**
R. **Lord, have mercy.**

V. **Christ, have mercy.**
R. **Christ, have mercy.**

V. **Lord, have mercy.**
R. **Lord, have mercy.**

Gloria

When the Gloria is sung or said, the priest or everyone together may say:

**Glory to God in the highest,
    and peace to his people
    on earth.
Lord God, heavenly King, almighty God and Father,
    we worship you, we give you
        thanks,
    we praise you for your glory.
Lord Jesus Christ, only Son of
    the Father,
Lord God, Lamb of God.
You take away the sin of the
    world:
        have mercy on us;
you are seated at the right hand
    of the Father:
        receive our prayer.
For you alone are the Holy One,
you alone are the Lord,
you alone are the Most High,**

Jesus Christ,
with the Holy Spirit,
in the glory of God the Father.
> Amen.

Opening Prayer
Priest: **Let us pray.**
Then the priest says the opening prayer which gives the theme of the day's celebration. He concludes:
Priest: **...forever and ever.**
People: **Amen.**

LITURGY OF THE WORD

We listen to God's message from Holy Scripture as proclaimed by his prophets and apostles.

First Reading
At the end of the reading:
Reader: **The Word of the Lord.**

People: **Thanks be to God.**
Responsorial Psalm
The people repeat the response said by the reader the first time and then after each verse.

Second Reading
At the end of the reading:
Reader: **The Word of the Lord.**

People: **Thanks be to God.**

Alleluia
The people repeat the Alleluia after the reader's Alleluia and then after the verse.

Gospel
Deacon (or Priest): **The Lord be with you.**
People: **And also with you.**
Deacon (or Priest): **A reading from the gospel according to N.**
People: **Glory to you, Lord.**
At the end of the reading:
Deacon (or Priest): **The gospel of the Lord.**
People: **Praise to you, Lord Jesus Christ.**

Homily
We have heard God's message, and now we listen to the words spoken by the priest about God's message.

Profession of Faith
We express our faith in God
We believe in one God,
>   the Father, the Almighty,
>   maker of heaven and earth,
>   of all that is seen and unseen.

We believe in one Lord, Jesus Christ,
>   the only Son of God,
>   eternally begotten of the Father,
>
> God from God, Light from Light,
> true God from true God,
>   begotten, not made, one in Being with the Father.

Through him all things were made.
For us men and for our salvation
>   he came down from heaven:

by the power of the Holy Spirit.
(All bow at the following words up to: **and became man.)**

he was born of the Virgin
Mary, and became man.
For our sake he was crucified
under Pontius Pilate:
he suffered, died, and was
buried.
On the third day he rose again
in fulfillment of the Scriptures;
he ascended into heaven
and is seated at the right
hand of the Father.
He will come again in glory to
judge the living and the dead,
and his kingdom will have no
end.
We believe in the Holy Spirit,
the Lord, the giver of life,
who proceeds from the Father
and the Son.
With the Father and the Son
he is worshiped and glorified.
He has spoken through the
Prophets.

We believe in one holy catholic
 and apostolic Church.
We acknowledge one baptism
 for the forgiveness of sins.
We look for the resurrection
 of the dead,
and the life of the world to
 come. Amen.

General Intercessions
(Prayer of the Faithful)
We unite with one another to pray for our needs, for the whole Church and people everywhere. After the priest gives the introduction, the deacon or other minister sings or says the invocations.
People: **Lord, hear our prayer.**
(or other response, according to local customs)
At the end the priest says the concluding prayer:
People: **Amen.**

LITURGY OF THE EUCHARIST

Offertory Song
We bring bread and wine for the Sacrifice. Before placing the bread on the altar, the priest says quietly:
Blessed are you, Lord, God of all creation.
Through your goodness we have this bread to offer,
which earth has given and human hands have made.
It will become for us the bread of life.

If there is no singing, the people respond:
People: **Blessed be God for ever.**

Before placing the chalice on the altar, the priest says:

**Blessed are you, God of
    all creation.
Through your goodness we have
    this wine to offer,
fruit of the vine and work of
    human hands.
It will become our spiritual
    drink.**

If there is no singing, the people respond:
People: **Blessed be God for ever.**

Invitation to Prayer
Priest: **Pray, brethren, that our sacrifice may be acceptable to God, the almighty Father.**

People: **May the Lord accept the sacrifice at your hands for the praise and glory of his name, for our good and the good of all his Church.**

Prayer Over the Gifts
At the end:
People: **Amen.**

EUCHARISTIC PRAYER

The priest offers the great Sacrifice.

Introductory dialogue

Priest: **The Lord be with you.**
People: **And also with you.**
Priest: **Lift up your hearts.**
People: **We lift them up to the Lord.**

Priest: **Let us give thanks to the Lord our God.**
People: **It is right to give him thanks and praise.**

Preface

Praise to the Father

**Father, it is our duty and our salvation,
always and everywhere
to give you thanks
through your beloved Son, Jesus Christ.
He is the Word through whom you made the universe,
the Savior you sent to redeem us.
By the power of the Holy Spirit
he took flesh and was born of the Virgin Mary.
For our sake he opened his arms on the cross;
he put an end to death
and revealed the resurrection.
In this he fulfilled your will
and won for you a holy people.**

And so we join the angels and the saints
in proclaiming your glory
as we sing (say):

Sanctus
First Acclamation of the People
Priest and People:
Holy, holy, holy Lord, God of power and might,
heaven and earth are full of your glory.
Hosanna in the highest.
Blessed is he who comes in the name of the Lord.
Hosanna in the highest.

Invocation of the Holy Spirit

Lord, you are holy indeed,
 the fountain of all holiness.
Let your Spirit come upon these
 gifts to make them holy,
so that they may become for us
the body and blood of our Lord,
 Jesus Christ.

The Lord's Supper

Before he was given up to death,
 a death he freely accepted,
he took bread and gave you thanks.
He broke the bread,
gave it to his disciples, and said:
Take this, all of you, and eat it:
this is my body which will be
 given up for you.

When supper was ended, he took the cup.
Again he gave you thanks and praise,
gave the cup to his disciples, and said:
Take this, all of you, and drink from it:
this is the cup of my blood,
the blood of the new and everlasting covenant.
It will be shed for you and for all
so that sins may be forgiven.
Do this in memory of me.

Memorial Acclamation

Priest: Let us proclaim the mystery of faith:
People: Christ has died,
Christ is risen,
Christ will come again.
(or)
**Dying you destroyed our death,
rising you restored our life,
Lord Jesus, come in glory.**
(or)
**When we eat this bread and drink this cup,
we proclaim your death, Lord Jesus,
until you come in glory.**
(or)
**Lord, by your cross and resurrection
You have set us free.
You are the Savior of the world.**

The Memorial Prayer

**In memory of his death and
 resurrection,
we offer you, Father, this
 life-giving bread,
 this saving cup.
We thank you for counting us
 worthy
to stand in your presence and
 serve you.**

Invocation of the Holy Spirit

**May all of us who share in the
 body and blood of Christ
be brought together in unity by
 the Holy Spirit.**

Intercessions: For the Church

Lord, remember your Church
    throughout the world:
make us grow in love,
together with N. our Pope,
N. our bishop, and all the clergy.

For the Dead

Remember our brothers and sisters
who have gone to their rest
in the hope of rising again;
bring them and all the departed
into the light of your presence.

In Communion with the Saints

Have mercy on us all;
make us worthy to share eternal
    life

with Mary, the virgin Mother of
 God,
 with the apostles,
and with all the saints who have
 done your will throughout the
 ages.
May we praise you in union
 with them,
and give you glory
through your Son, Jesus Christ.

Concluding Doxology
Through him,
with him,
in him,
in the unity of the Holy Spirit,
all glory and honor is yours,
almighty Father,
for ever and ever.

All reply: **Amen.**

COMMUNION RITE

The Lord's Prayer
Priest: **Let us pray with confidence to the Father in the words our Savior gave us:**

Priest and people: **Our Father, who art in heaven, hallowed be thy name; thy kingdom come; thy will be done on earth as it is in heaven. Give us this day our daily bread; and forgive us our trespasses as we forgive those who trespass against us; and lead us not into temptation, but deliver from evil.**

Priest: **Deliver us, Lord, from every evil,
and grant us peace in our day.
In your mercy keep us free from sin
and protect us from all anxiety
as we wait in joyful hope
for the coming of our Saviour,
Jesus Christ.**

People: **For the kingdom, the power, and the glory are yours, now and for ever.**

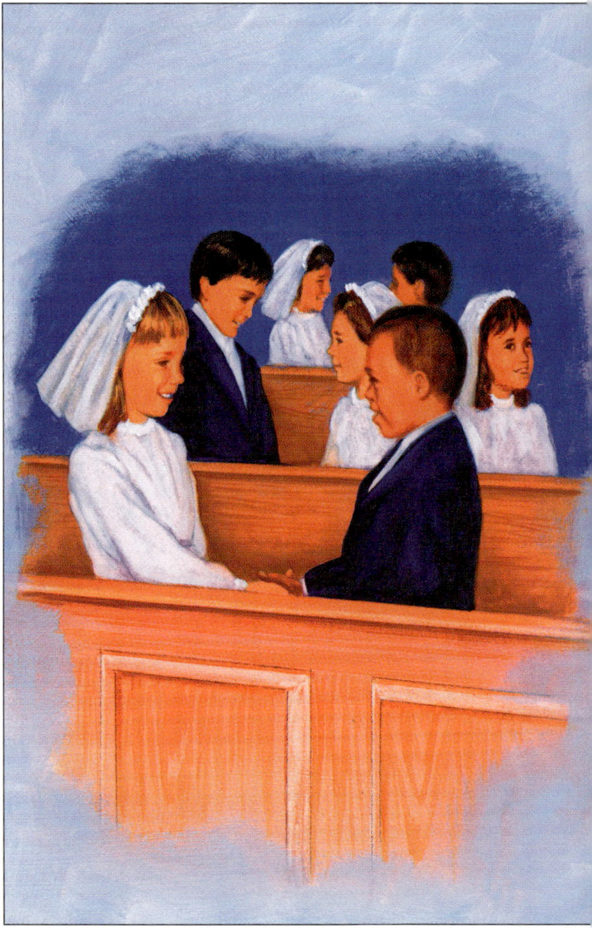

Sign of Peace

(The priest says the prayer for peace and concludes: **for ever and ever.***)*

People: **Amen.**
Priest: **The peace of the Lord be with you always.**
People: **And also with you.**
Deacon (or Priest):
Let us offer each other the sign of peace.
(The people exchange a sign of peace and love, according to local custom.)

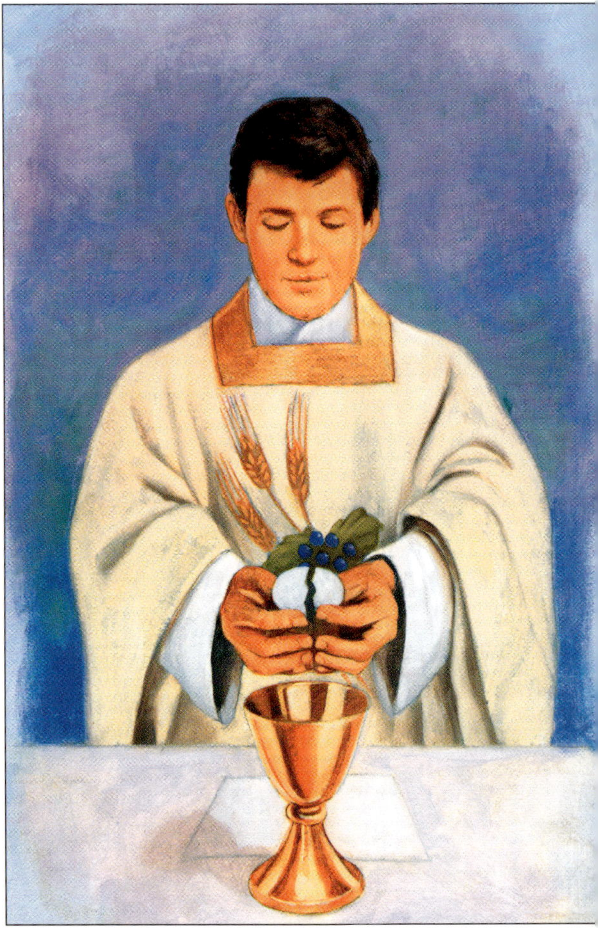

Breaking of the Bread
(The people sing or say:)
Lamb of God, you take away the sins of the world:
   have mercy on us.
Lamb of God, you take away the sins of the world:
   have mercy on us.
Lamb of God, you take away the sins of the world:
   grant us peace.
(Then the priest joins his hands and says quietly:)
Lord Jesus Christ, Son of the Living God,
by the will of the Father and the work of the Holy Spirit
your death brought life to the world.
By your holy body and blood
free me from all my sins and from every evil.

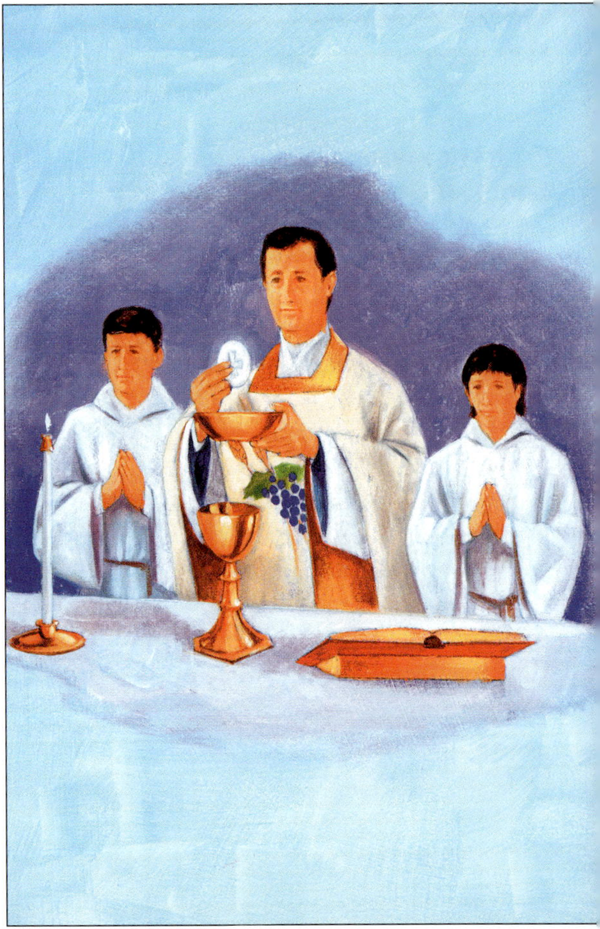

**Keep me faithful to your teaching,
and never let me be parted from
   you.**
(or)
**Lord Jesus Christ,
with faith in your love and mercy
I eat your body and drink your
   blood.
Let it not bring me
   condemnation,
but health in mind and body.**

Communion
Priest: **This is the Lamb of God
who takes away the sins of
world.
        Happy are those who are
called to his supper.**
Priest and people: **Lord, I am not
   worthy to receive you,
but only say the word and I shall
   be healed.**

Communion of the Priest

The priest says quietly:
**May the body of Christ bring
   me to everlasting life.**
*He reverently consumes the body of Christ.
The priest then takes the chalice and says in a low voice:*
**May the blood of Christ bring
   me to everlasting life.**
He reverently drinks the blood of Christ.

Communion of the People

Priest: **The Body of Christ.**
Communicant: **Amen.**
During or after Communion there may be a period of silence or a song of praise may be sung.

Prayer after Communion
Priest: **Let us pray.**
Everyone prays silently for a while. Then the priest says the prayer after Communion. The people respond:
People: **Amen.**

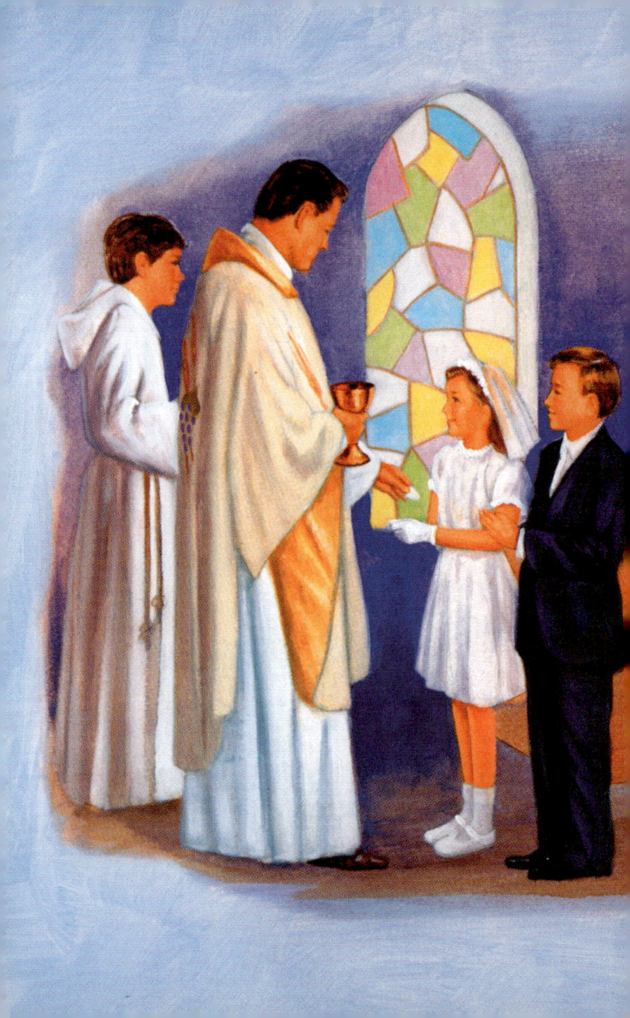

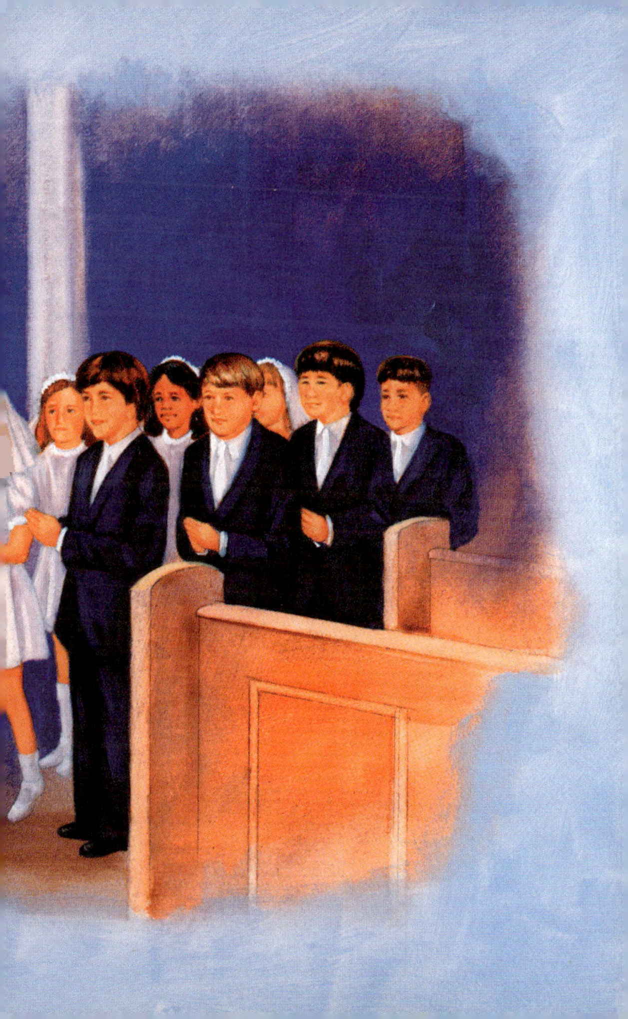

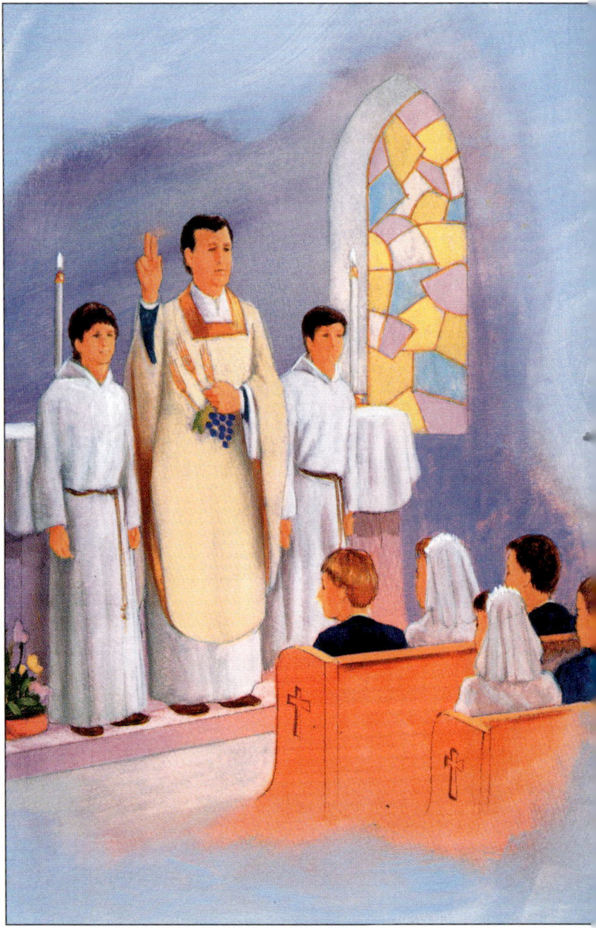

CONCLUDING RITE

Now it is time for us to leave, to do good works, to praise and bless the Lord in our daily lives.
After any announcements, the blessing and dismissal follow.

Blessing
Priest: **The Lord be with you.**
People: **And also with you.**
Priest: **May almighty God bless you, the Father, and the Son,☨ and the Holy Spirit.**
People: **Amen.**
Dismissal
Deacon (or Priest):
> **Go in the peace of Christ:**
> > *(or)*
>
> **The Mass has ended, go in peace.**
> > *(or)*
>
> **Go in peace to love and serve the Lord.**

People: **Thanks be to God.**

THE CHURCH YEAR

The seasons of the Church are: Advent, Christmas, Lent, Easter, Pentecost and Ordinary Time.

Advent means coming. Each year for four weeks before Christmas, Christians prepare their minds and hearts for the birth of Jesus.

The six weeks before Easter are called Lent. For Christians, Lent is a time of special prayer, reflection and self-denial. The first Easter was the day Jesus fulfilled his promise and arose from the dead.

Pentecost celebrates the days the disciples were gathered together and the Holy Spirit entered them. The spirit gave them the courage to be like Jesus.

During the remaining weeks, a season called Ordinary Time, the Church invites us to learn more about Jesus and his Spirit in us.

FAVORITE GOSPEL STORIES

The Gospels read at Mass are stories from the life of Jesus. They are chosen in accordance with the seasons of the Church Year. The Gospels rotate on a three year schedule: Cycle A, Cycle B and Cycle C.

The following selection is a brief introduction to the Church's large number of Gospels. Read these and other stories from the New Testament as often as you can.

Always be attentive and listen carefully during Mass. The more Gospel stories you read and hear, the closer you will be drawn to Jesus; and he will send the Holy Spirit to fill your heart with love and wisdom.

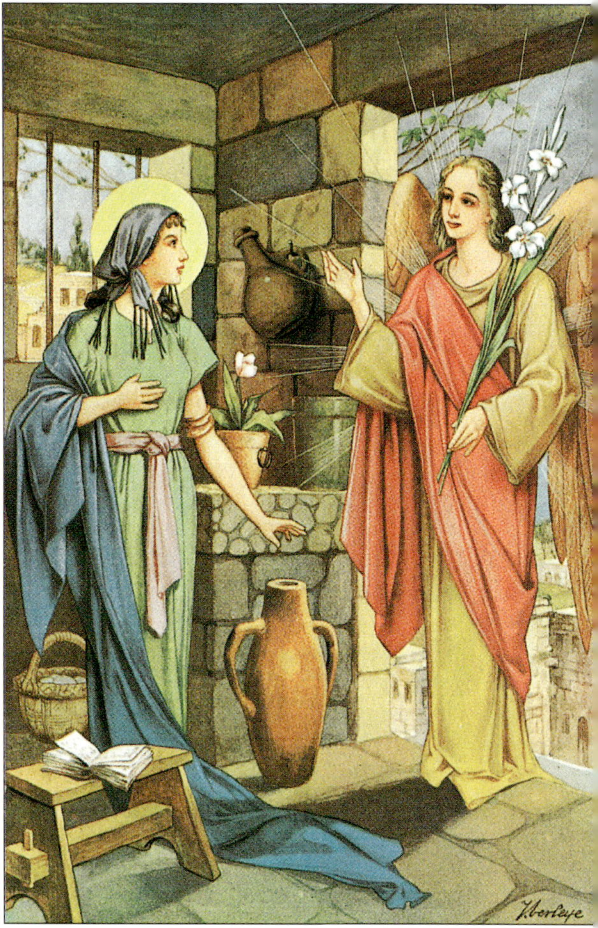

J. Verleye

AN ANGEL SPEAKS TO MARY

In Nazareth, there lived a young woman named Mary, who was engaged to Joseph, a carpenter, and an angel of the Lord came to her with a message. "Do not be afraid, Mary," said the Angel. God has sent me to tell you that you will be the mother of a son, and his name will be Jesus."

Mary was surprised, but the Angel said, "The Holy Spirit will come to you, and your child shall be called the Son of God. He shall rule a kingdom that will last forever."

And Mary said, "I am God's servant. I will do what he asks."

And the Angel went away.

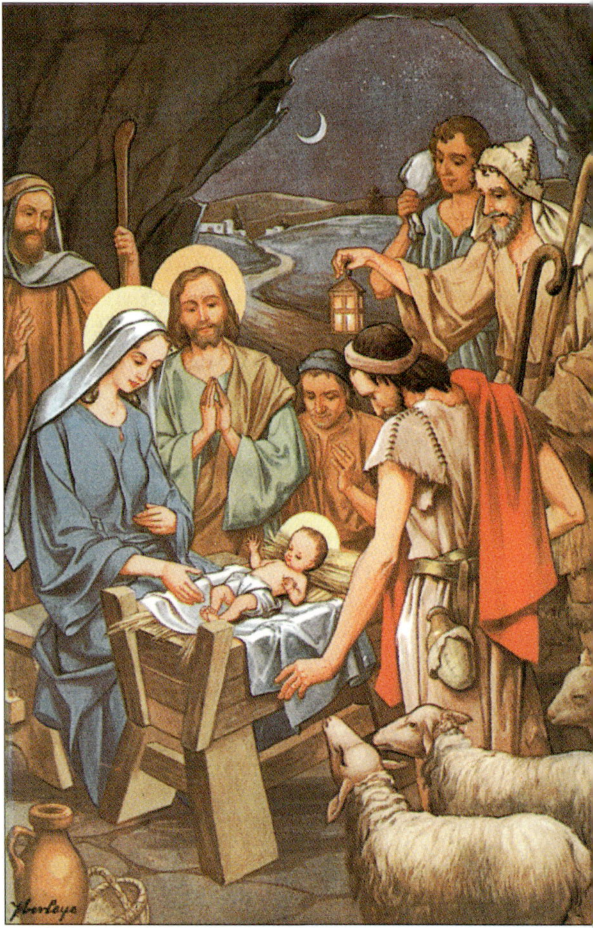

JESUS IS BORN

In time Mary and Joseph, her husband, went to Bethlehem. But the town was crowded and they had to sleep in a cave. Mary's baby, Jesus, was born there that night.

Nearby an angel came to some shepherds who were watching their sheep, and he said, "A child has been born in Bethlehem. He is Christ the Lord." And many angels sang:

"Glory to God in the highest,
 And peace on earth."

The shepherds went to Bethlehem to see the child and they found him with Mary and Joseph. Then the shepherds went away praising God.

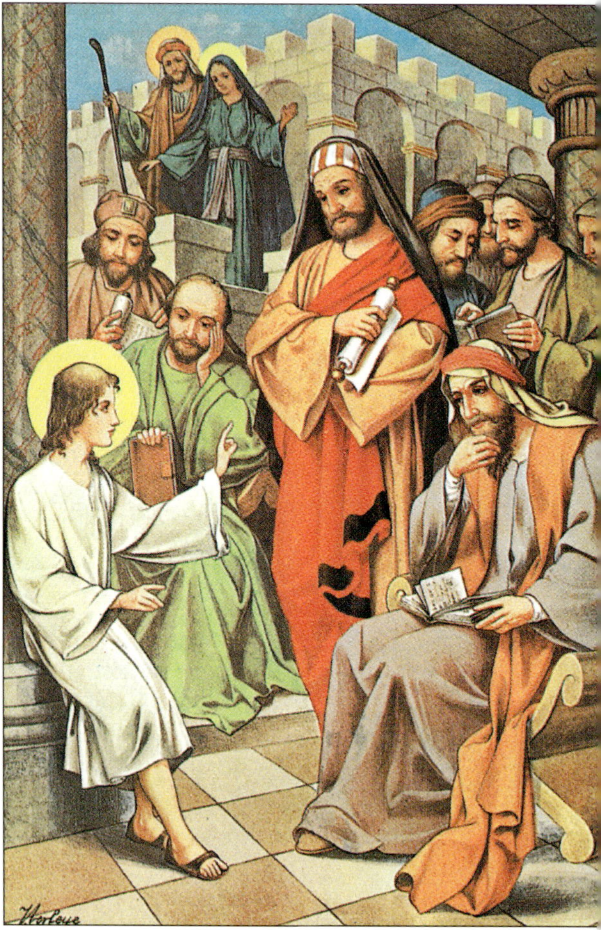

THE CHILD JESUS IN THE TEMPLE

After a holiday, Mary and Joseph were returning home to Nazareth with their friends and twelve-year-old Jesus. At first Mary thought Jesus was with another family, but when she learned he was not, she and Joseph went back to Jerusalem to look for him. They searched for three days before they found him in the temple. He was talking with teachers who were amazed at his knowledge of God's teachings.

Mary asked, "Son, why have you worried us so?" Jesus answered, "Didn't you know that I must do my Father's work?" But he went home with Mary and Joseph and obeyed them.

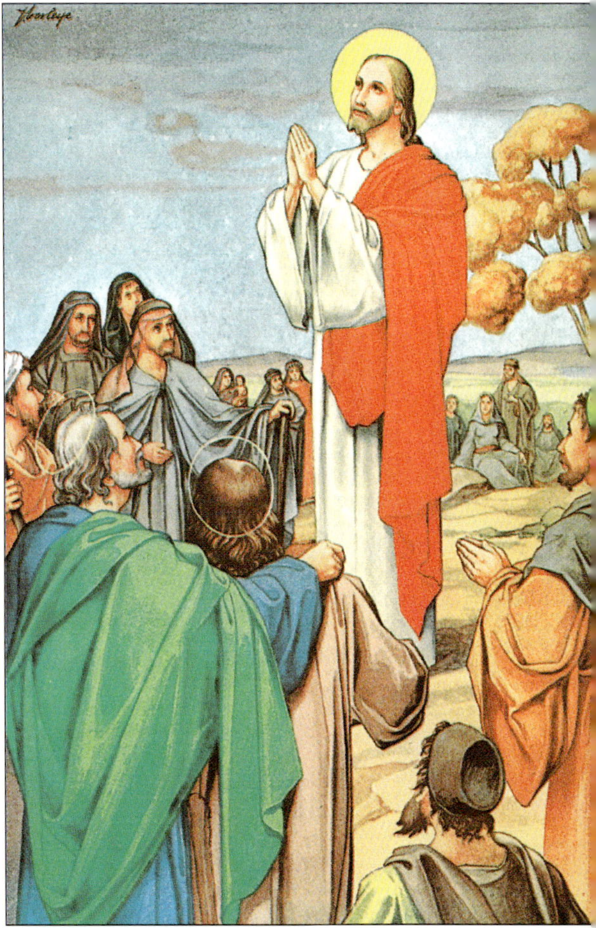

JESUS SPEAKS TO THE PEOPLE

One day Jesus went to a mountain top, and he spoke to the people. He said, "Love everyone, even those who are not kind to you. Treat others as you want them to treat you. Ask God your Father for whatever you need. Here is how you are to pray to him:

'Our father who art in heaven, hallowed be thy name. Thy kingdom come, thy will be done on earth as it is in heaven. Give us this day our daily bread. And forgive us our trespasses, as we forgive those who trespass against us. And lead us not into temptation, but deliver us from evil."

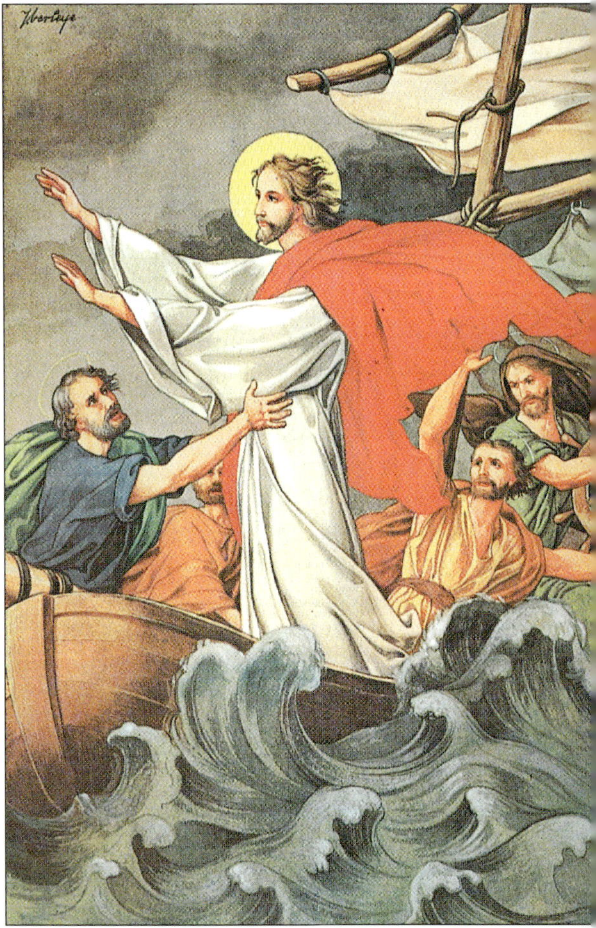

A STORM ON THE LAKE

One evening Jesus said to his apostles, "Let us sail to the other side of the lake." When their boat was out on the water, a storm arose. Winds blew and waves beat against the sides of the little vessel. But Jesus had fallen asleep.

The apostles woke him and cried, "Master save us or we shall drown!" And Jesus stood and said to the sea, "Peace. Be still." At once the winds fell and the sea grew calm. And Jesus asked the apostles, "Why were you afraid?" And they said to one another, "Who is this Jesus? Even the wind and the waves obey him."

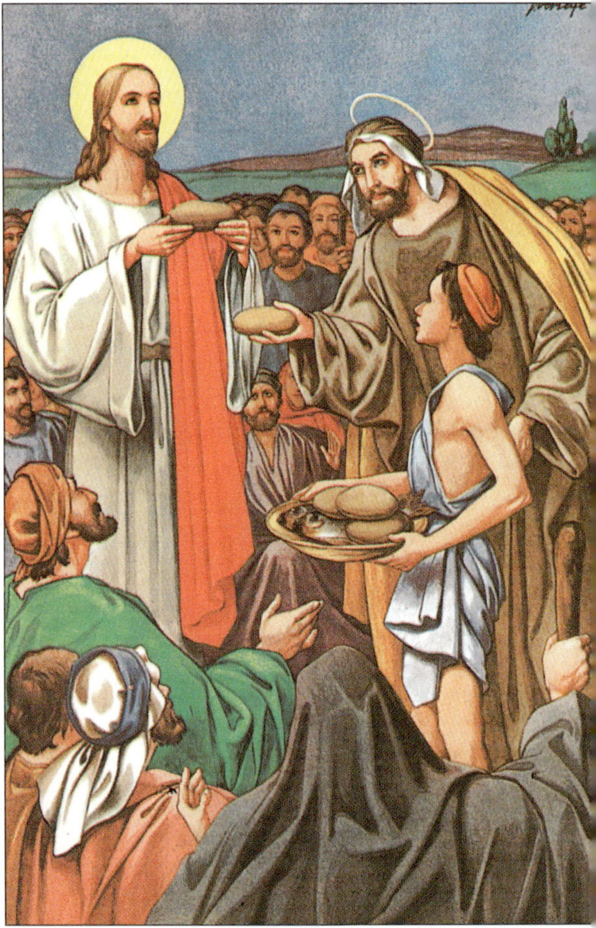

JESUS FEEDS THE PEOPLE

A crowd had followed Jesus all day, and in the evening the apostles said, "The people are hungry." And the apostle Philip announced, "A boy is here with five loaves of bread and two fishes, but that is not enough for so many." But Jesus said, "Let the people sit down." After the five thousand were seated on the grass, Jesus blessed the loaves and fishes, and the apostles handed them to the crowd. And when everyone had eaten, they picked up what was left, and the food filled twelve baskets. The people were amazed that Jesus had fed so many with so little food.

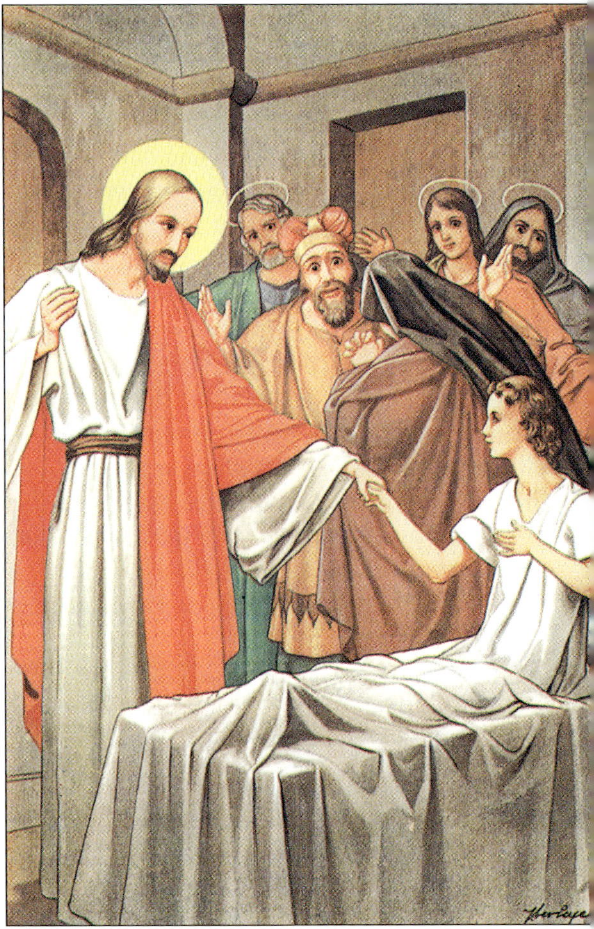

A YOUNG GIRL LIVES AGAIN

As Jesus was speaking, one of the rulers came and knelt before Him and said: "Lord, my daughter has just died; come, lay your hand on her, and she will live again." So Jesus rose up and followed the ruler, and so did the apostles.

When Jesus came into the ruler's house, He found mourners weeping. He said: "Make room. The child is not dead. She is asleep." And they laughed aloud at Him. But when the multitude had moved away, He went in and took the girl by the hand, and she arose. The story of these doings spread abroad through all the country round.

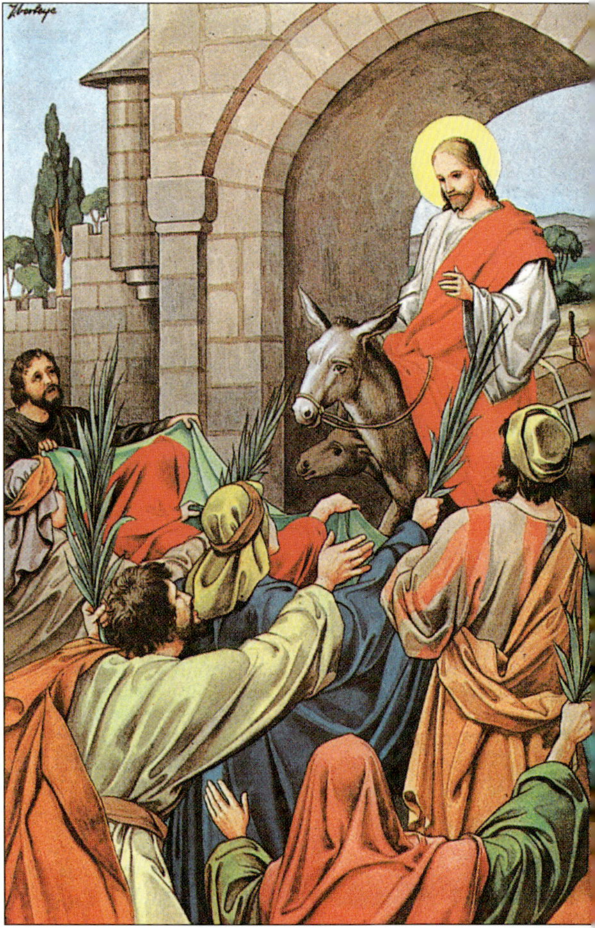

JESUS ENTERS JERUSALEM

When Jesus was near Jerusalem, two of his friends brought him a young donkey, and Jesus sat upon it to ride into the city. Many people threw their coats on the road in front of him, and others cut branches from trees and cast them in his path to show their love for Jesus. Then those who marched before him began to praise God for the wonderful things Jesus had done for them and for all he had taught them. They shouted:

"Blessed is he who comes as king
in the name of the Lord!
Hosanna to the Son of David!
Glory in the highest!"

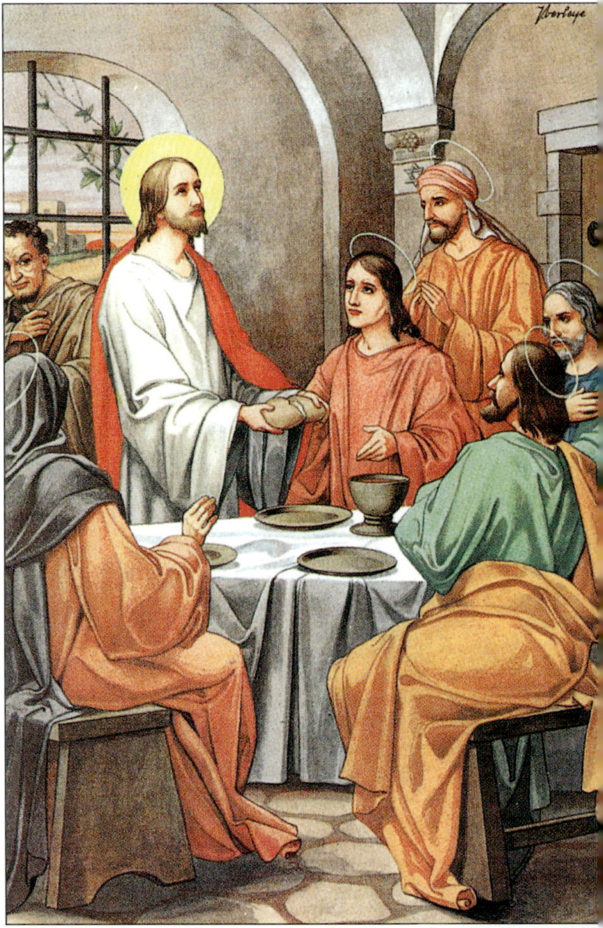

THE LAST SUPPER

On Holy Thursday, Jesus washed the feet of his apostles and then sat down to eat supper with them. During the meal, he took the bread and gave it to the apostles and said, "Take this and eat; it is my body." Then he took a cup of wine and said, "Drink this; it is my blood."

And he said to his apostles, "Love one another as I love you. Soon I will leave you to go to my Father. But I will send the Holy Spirit who will live with you and teach you what you need to know."

Then Jesus and the apostles sang a hymn and prayed together.

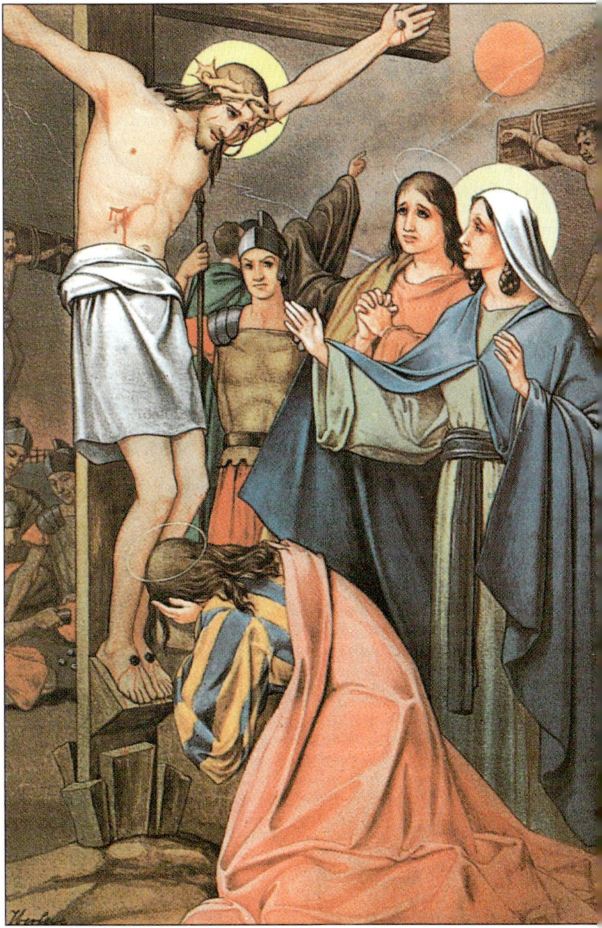

JESUS IS PUT TO DEATH

Men in power hated Jesus because he had said he was the Son of God. Now Judas, the apostle, did an evil act. He told the enemies of Jesus where to find him, and on Holy Thursday they arrested him. When the judges asked him if he was truly the Son of God, Jesus would not deny it. Then he was flogged, and the soldiers put a crown of thorns on his head because the people had called him their king.

On Good Friday Jesus was taken to Golgotha and nailed to a cross, and there he died. His friends took down his body, wrapped it in a sheet, and buried it in a cave.

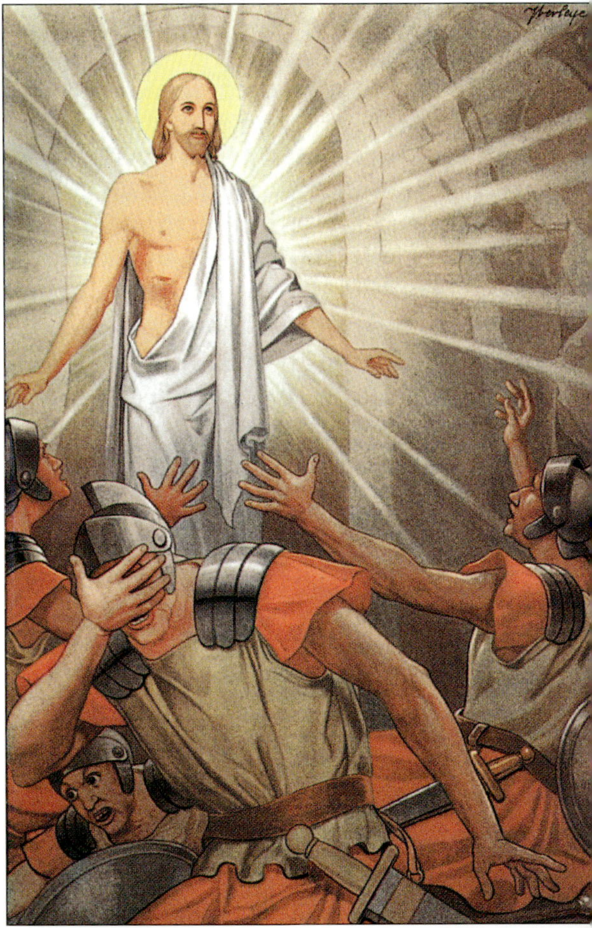

EASTER

On Easter morning, some women went to the tomb where Jesus lay, to put spices on his body. Suddenly they remembered that a heavy stone had been rolled in front of the tomb. One woman said, "Who will roll away the stone for us?" But when they got there it had already been rolled away, and a man in white robes was sitting in the tomb. He said, "Do not be afraid. Jesus has risen from the dead. Tell Peter and the other apostles." As the women ran off, they saw Jesus, and they knelt to adore him. And he said, "Tell the apostles to wait for me in Galilee."

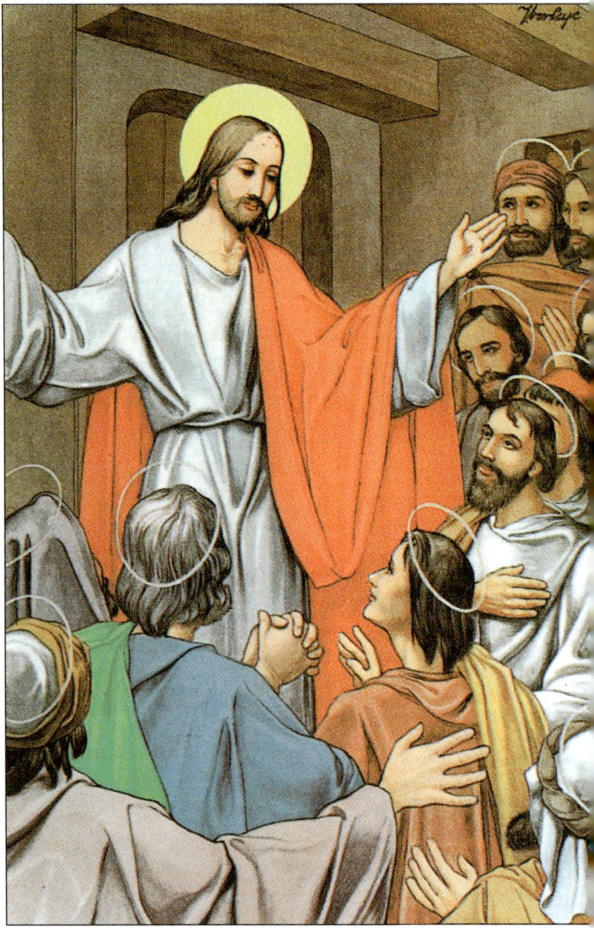

THE APOSTLES SEE THE RISEN JESUS

The apostles were indoors when Jesus came to them and said, "Peace be with you." He showed them his wounded hands. But Thomas, one of the apostles, was not there, and when they told him they had seen Jesus, he said, "I do not believe it. If I can put my fingers in his wounds, I will believe he is risen."

Again Jesus came, and when he saw Thomas he said, "Put your fingers into my wounds." But Thomas said, "My Lord and my God." And Jesus said, "You believe because you see me. Blessed are people who do not see me and who believe."

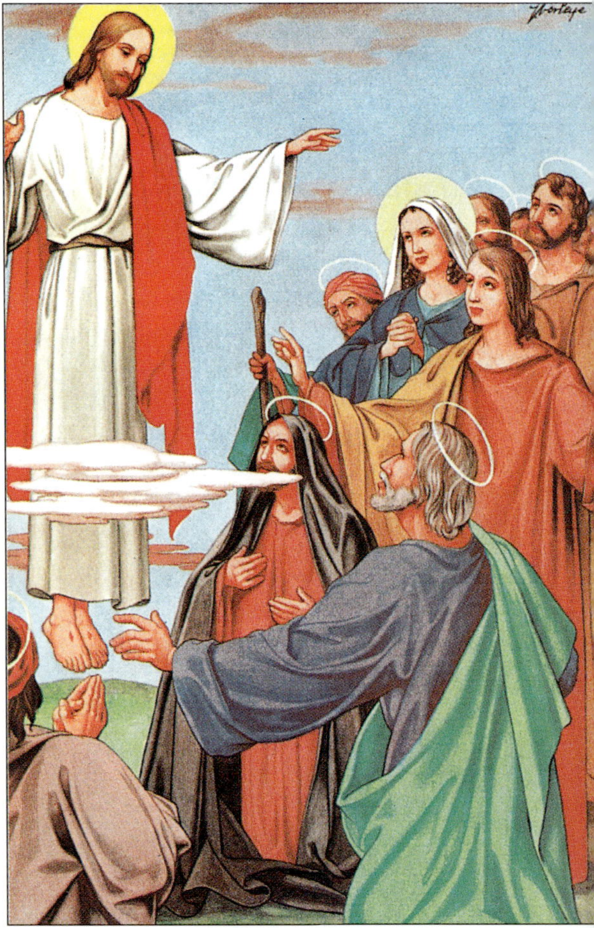

THE ASCENSION

After Jesus rose from the dead, he stayed on earth for forty days, visiting his apostles and talking to them. He said to them, "Go and teach all people what I have taught you. But wait in Jerusalem until I send you the Holy Spirit." After that, Jesus led them to Mount Olivet and blessed them. Then he rose slowly toward the sky until a cloud hid him from sight. As they kept looking up two men in white appeared and said, "Men of Galilee, why do you stand gazing up at the sky? Jesus, who has gone to heaven, will return again."

And the apostles went back to Jerusalem.

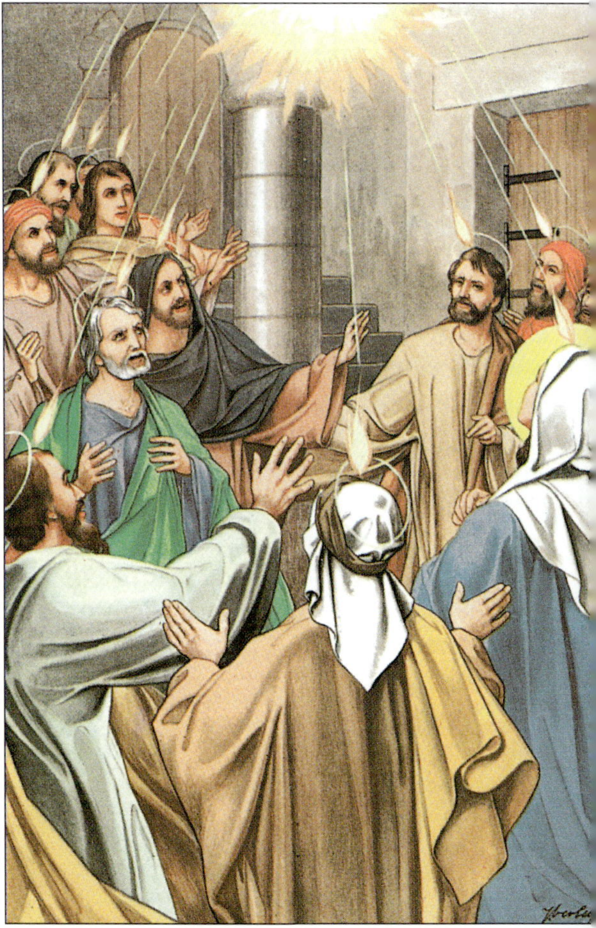

THE COMING OF THE HOLY SPIRIT

The apostles, Mary, the mother of Jesus, and their friends prayed and waited for the coming of the Holy Spirit. Then, one day, they heard a sound like the wind, and tongues of fire settled on them. All were filled with the Holy Spirit and they began to speak in many languages. Now visitors from other lands were in Jerusalem, and when the apostles began to speak, the visitors said, "How is it that, no matter what countries we come from, we hear the apostles speaking in our own languages?" The apostles told the story of God's son and great numbers believed in Jesus and became his followers.

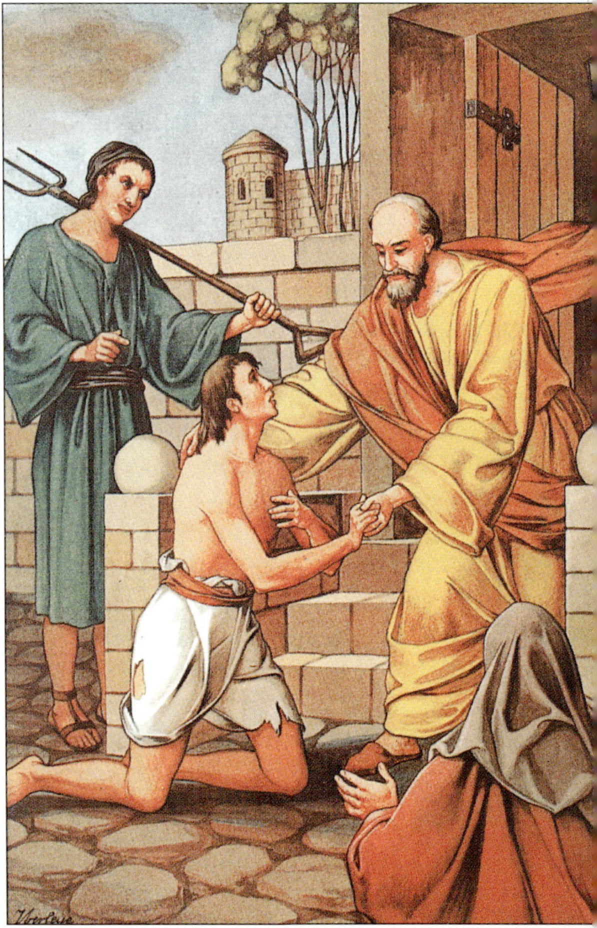

THE LOVING FATHER

A young man left home and went to live in a far place where he spent his money foolishly. When it was all gone, he took a job caring for pigs, but the pigs had more to eat than he had, and he said, "The men who work for my father always have enough food. I will go home and ask if I may work for him." He walked along and when his father saw him, he ran to the son and kissed him. And the son said, "Father, I am not worthy to be your son," But the father said to a servant, "Prepare a feast so that we may celebrate my son's return home."

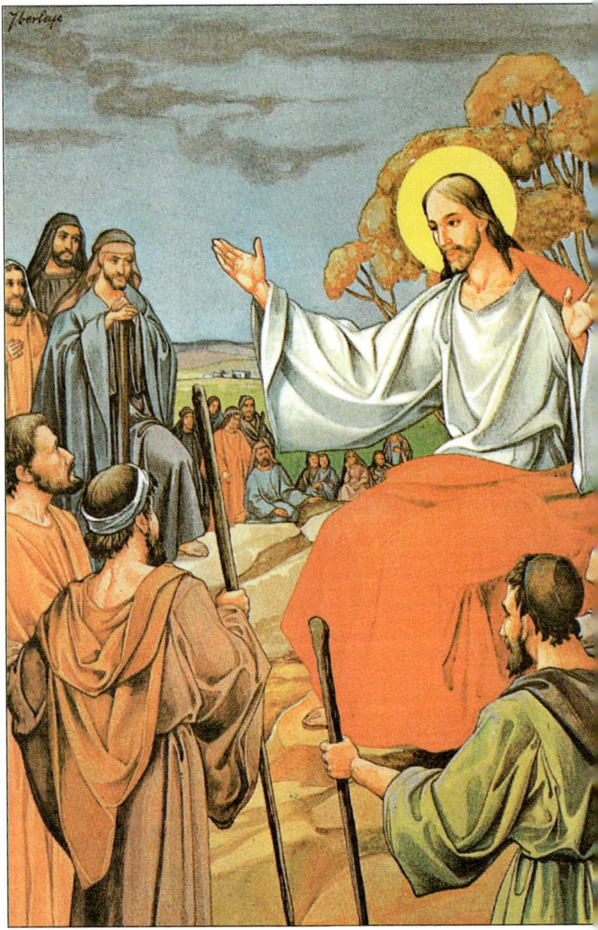
Iberlaye

THE SERMON ON THE MOUNT

Jesus, seeing the multitude, began speaking to them, saying: Blessed are the poor in spirit: the reign of God is theirs. Blessed are the sorrowing: they shall be consoled. Blessed are the lowly: they shall inherit the land. Blessed are they who hunger and thirst for holiness: they shall have their fill. Blessed are they who show mercy: mercy shall be theirs. Blessed are the pure in heart: they shall see God. Blessed are the peacemakers: they shall be called sons and daughters of God. Blessed are those persecuted for justice' sake: the reign of God is theirs. Blessed are you when men shall reproach you and speak evil against you falsely because of me; be glad and rejoice, for your reward will be very great in heaven.

RECONCILIATION

Jesus has asked us to love God with with all our heart, all our mind and all our soul; and to love our neighbor as ourself.

Sometimes we do not follow Jesus and we fail to love as we should. This separates us from God. It is the way we sin.

But Jesus loves us too much to let us remain apart. He wants very much to forgive us if only we go to him, say we are sorry and promise to do better. This we do through the Sacrament of Reconciliation.

EXAMINATION OF CONSCIENCE

Before confessing your sins, it is important to look at your life and ask yourself some questions:

Have I behaved as God's child should?

Do I pray to God every day?

Have I given trouble to my parents and teachers?

Have I been selfish in my dealings with others?

Have I been honest and truthful?

Have I quarreled and not tried to make friends again?

Have I neglected my work in school or at home?

Do I respect my body and take good care of it?

Do I help those who are poor or handicapped or have other needs?

Do I show the old, the sick or the lonely that I care about them?

When going to confession, either in the Reconciliation Room or behind the confessional screen, always remember that the priest represents Jesus. There is no need to be afraid. The priest is there to help you. He will show you how to let Jesus come into your life.

RECEIVING THE SACRAMENT

After you greet the priest, make the Sign of the Cross. The priest may read a passage from Holy Scripture. If he does, listen carefully to God's Word.

You will then speak to the priest about your sins. Tell him whatever is keeping you away from God and preventing you from being a better follower of Jesus.

When you are finished, the priest will counsel you and may ask you to say a prayer or do something to show your sorrow. He may ask you to recite an Act of Contrition.

ACT OF CONTRITION

O my God, I am heartily sorry for having offended you and I detest all my sins, because of your just punishments, but most of all because they offend you, my God, who are all good and deserving of all my love. I firmly resolve, with the help of your grace, to sin no more and to avoid the near occasions of sin. Amen.

Then the priest will say the words of absolution and reconciliation.

When you leave, remember to thank the priest. Then remain a few minutes in church and tell Jesus how happy and grateful you are because your sins are forgiven.

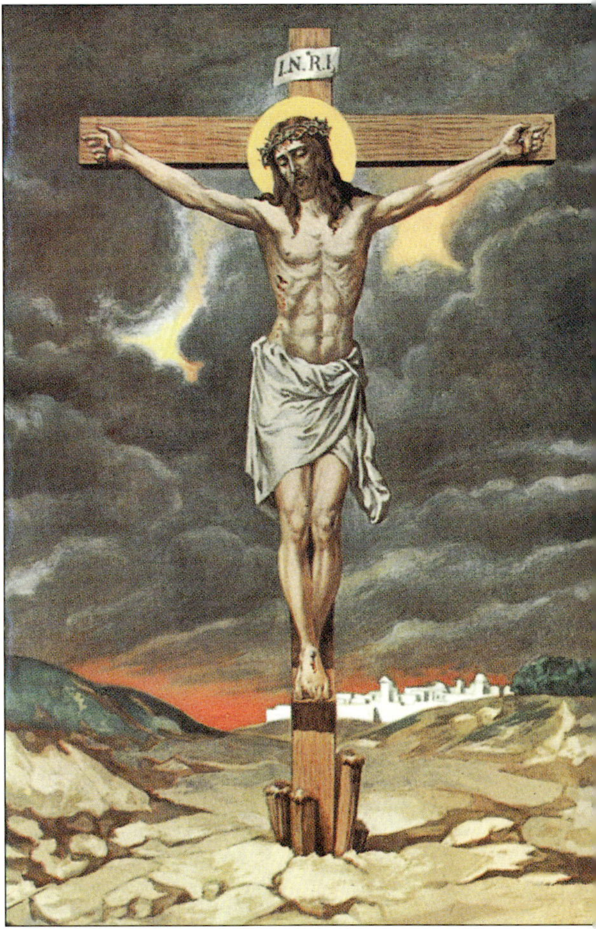
I.N.R.I.

THE STATIONS OF THE CROSS

Each Good Friday, we recall the passion of Jesus, the day he suffered and died on the cross.

On the first Good Friday, almost 2000 years ago, Jesus made many stops on the way to Calvary. The fourteen pictures around the walls of our church remind us of all that happened on that sad day.

A good way to thank Jesus is to visit each station, think of what happened and tell Jesus how much we love him.

First Station
JESUS MEETS PILATE

Jesus' first stop on the way of the cross is the Governor's palace. Many Jewish leaders wanted Jesus out of the way. "Crucify him," they insisted. And they influenced Pilate the Governor to condemn Jesus to death.

Second Station
JESUS TAKES THE CROSS

The Roman Soldiers bring a large wooden cross for Jesus to carry. It is very heavy and rough. Though Jesus is tired, sick, and weak, he reaches out and accepts the cross lovingly. By his love he transforms this cross into a symbol of hope and salvation for all people.

Third Station
JESUS FALLS

Soon after he begins to carry the cross, Jesus falls. He is very exhausted and the weight of the cross crushes him. The soldiers roughly drag him to his feet and Jesus slowly continues his painful journey.

Fourth Station
JESUS MEETS HIS MOTHER

On the narrow roadway, Jesus turns the corner and looks ahead to see his mother. She reaches out to touch him. He is thankful that she is there. She doesn't say anything to him, but he knows that she loves him even though she feels sad and helpless to do anything.

Fifth Station
SIMON HELPS JESUS

The soldiers notice that Jesus is very weak. He is staggering under the load, so they pull a man from the crowd -a stranger- and force him to help Jesus carry his cross. The stranger, whose name is Simon Cyrene, is frightened and doesn't know who Jesus is.

Sixth Station
VERONICA WIPES JESUS' FACE

A woman named Veronica steps out from the crowd with a towel. Jesus' hands are holding his cross, so she wipes his face, which is dripping with blood and sweat. Veronica does a simple act of kindness to show she cares.

Seventh Station
JESUS FALLS AGAIN

The soldiers let Simon go his way and Jesus is again carrying the cross by himself. There is still a long way to go. Jesus staggers and falls. He is breathing very heavily and has no strength left. Yet he stands up. And because of his strong love, he is able to go forward.

Eighth Station
JESUS MEETS SOME WOMEN

Jesus meets a group of women from Jerusalem. They are weeping because he is suffering so much. Jesus tells them to weep for themselves and for their children, because the cruelty in the world will surely touch them just as it is touching him.

Ninth Station
JESUS FALLS A THIRD TIME

A third time Jesus falls. He has no more strength left. He has lost much blood and the hot sun burns his skin. Again he struggles to stand up because he has chosen the way of the cross out of love for us.

Tenth Station
JESUS IS STRIPPED

Jesus has reached the top of the hill. The soldiers let him drop the cross to the ground. And while Jesus stands there in front of the crowds, the soldiers pull off his clothes leaving him embarrassed and humiliated. He is being treated as a common criminal, as if he were a worthless human being.

Eleventh Station
JESUS IS NAILED TO THE CROSS

Now the soldiers make Jesus lie down on the cross. They stretch out his arms and fasten them with nails. They also nail his feet so that he is securely fastened to the cross. He cannot escape. Only his great love for us enables Jesus to bear his pain and suffering.

Twelfth Station
JESUS DIES

The cross is standing and Jesus is hanging on it. Time goes by very slowly, for Jesus is full of pain. But more important than the pain is his love for us and his willingness to die for us to be free from sin.

Thirteenth Station
JESUS IS PLACED IN MARY'S ARMS

After Jesus dies, a few friends gently take his body down from the cross and put it in the arms of his mother. She held Jesus like this when he was a baby, but now his body has no life left in it. Her heart is filled with sadness.

Fourteenth Station
JESUS IS BURIED

The final stopping place for Jesus on this sad day is a tomb. His friends place his body on the stone slab, wipe off the blood, wash his body clean, and cover it with cloth and nice-smelling spices. His friends and his mother touch his body for the last time before they leave.

A HAPPY ENDING

After we recall the Fourteen Stations, it is good to remember what follows Good Friday. Jesus' story does not end in sadness but in joy. He not only died, but on Easter Sunday he rose out of his tomb gloriously alive.

Jesus' Father, who is God, willed to allow Jesus to die out of love for us. He also willed to bring Jesus back to life so that in Jesus we would have no fear of death. Jesus will lead us through death to new life.

THE ROSARY

The rosary is a special way of praying to God that honors Mary, the Mother of Jesus. While reciting the prayers, you think about certain stories in the lives of Jesus and Mary. These stories are called mysteries: a mystery is a story about God.

Rosary beads are used to keep count of the prayers and mysteries. Recite the Apostles' Creed while you hold the crucifix, then one Our Father and three Hail Marys. After that, as you think about each mystery, recite the Our Father on the large bead, the Hail Mary on each of ten smaller beads and finish with a Glory Be. That makes one decade. The complete rosary consists of five decades. There are four sets of mysteries and five stories in each set.

THE JOYFUL MYSTERIES

1. The Coming of Jesus is Announced
2. Mary Visits Elizabeth
3. Jesus is Born
4. Jesus is Presented to God
5. Jesus is Found in the Temple

THE MYSTERIES OF LIGHT

1. Jesus' Baptism in the Jordan
2. The Wedding at Cana
3. Jesus' Proclamation of the Kingdom of God
4. Jesus' Transfiguration
5. Jesus' Institution of the Eucharist

THE SORROWFUL MYSTERIES

1. Jesus' Agony in the Garden
2. Jesus is Whipped
3. Jesus is Crowned with Thorns
4. Jesus Carries His Cross
5. Jesus Dies on the Cross

THE GLORIOUS MYSTERIES

1. Jesus Rises from His Tomb
2. Jesus Ascends to Heaven
3. The Holy Spirit Descends
4. Mary is Assumed into Heaven
5. Mary is Crowned in Heaven

THE SACRAMENTS

Christ instituted seven sacraments. They are outward visible signs of God's grace given at special moments in a person's life. They help us live our lives more fully.

BAPTISM

Baptism is also called christening. It is the first sacrament we receive, and makes us members of the church. It is performed by pouring water on a person's forehead, and saying "I baptize you in the name of the Father, and of the Son, and of the Holy Spirit. Amen."

CONFIRMATION

Confirmation bestows the special seal or mark of the Holy Spirit. It gives you the special spiritual energy to make Jesus known in the world, and the courage to live the way Jesus would like you to live.

HOLY EUCHARIST

Communion is often called the greatest sacrament because Christ himself is present in the consecrated bread and wine. The bread and wine are transformed into Christ's body and blood by the priest during Mass.

RECONCILIATION

This sacrament brings us God's forgiveness through the words of a priest. Reconciliation makes us holy and reconciles us with God and the Church. This used to be called "Penance" or "Confession."

ANOINTING OF THE SICK

This sacrament is for the seriously ill, the infirm and the very old. The sacrament of the sick sanctifies sufferings, increases grace, forgives sins and makes us ready for heaven.

HOLY ORDERS

This sacrament gives priests the power to forgive sins, the power to anoint the sick, the power to change bread and wine into the body and blood of Christ, and the power to perpetuate Jesus' sacrifice, which is the Mass. Through Holy Orders, priests and bishops receive the Spirit's grace to guide the church and take care of the people of God.

MATRIMONY

This sacrament is received when a husband and wife pronounce their marriage vows. It gives the grace for two people to join their lives together until death. The husband and wife perform this sacrament for each other. The priest is only the official church witness of this sacrament. Matrimony also enables people to be good mothers and fathers.

THE TEN COMMANDMENTS

1. I am the Lord your God. You shall not have strange gods before me.
2. You shall not take the Name of the Lord your God in vain.
3. Remember to keep holy the Lord's Day.
4. Honor your father and your mother.
5. You shall not kill.
6. You shall not commit adultery.
7. You shall not steal.
8. You shall not bear false witness against your neighbor.
9. You shall not covet your neighbor's wife.
10. You shall not covet your neighbor's goods.

THE PRECEPTS OF THE CHURCH

1. To attend Mass every Sunday and holy day of obligation.
2. To celebrate the Sacrament of Reconciliation at least once a year; and to receive Holy Communion during Easter time.
3. To study Catholic teaching in preparation for the Sacrament of Confirmation and then to continue our religious education.
4. To observe the marriage laws of the Church.
5. To strengthen and support the Church.
6. To do penance, including abstaining and fasting on the appointed days.
7. To join in the missionary spirit and apostolate of the Church.

MEMORY PRAYERS

To pray is to talk to God or to think about Him. Sometimes we pray in our own words and tell what is deep in our hearts. Other times we say the prayers known by all Catholics. Some of these prayers are listed below. You should memorize them so you can say them at any time of the day or night.

THE SIGN OF THE CROSS

In the name of the Father
and of the Son †
and of the Holy Spirit.
Amen.

THE OUR FATHER

Our Father, who art in heaven, hallowed be thy name; thy kingdom come; thy will be done on earth as it is in heaven. Give us this day our daily bread; and forgive us our trespasses as we forgive those who trespass against us and lead us not into temptation, but deliver us from evil. Amen.

THE HAIL MARY

Hail Mary, full of grace, the Lord is with thee. Blessed art thou amongst women, and blessed is the fruit of thy womb, Jesus. Holy Mary, Mother of God, pray for us sinners, now and at the hour of our death. Amen.

THE GLORY BE

Glory be to the Father, and to the Son, and to the Holy Spirit, as it was in the beginning, is now, and ever shall be, world without end. Amen.

THE APOSTLES' CREED

I believe in God, the Father almighty creator of heaven and earth. I believe in Jesus Christ, his only Son, our Lord. He was conceived by the power of the Holy Spirit and born of the Virgin Mary. He suffered under Pontius Pilate, was crucified, died, and was buried. He descended to the dead. On the third day he rose again. He ascended into heaven, and is seated at the right hand of the Father. He will come again to judge the living and the dead. I believe in the Holy Spirit, the holy Catholic Church, the communion of saints, the forgiveness of sins, the resurrection of the body, and the life everlasting. Amen.

ACT OF CONTRITION

My God, I am sorry for my sins with all my heart. In choosing to do wrong and failing to do good, I have sinned against you whom I should love above all things. I firmly intend with your help, to do penance, to sin no more, and to avoid whatever leads me to sin. Our Savior Jesus Christ suffered and died for us. In his name, my God, have mercy.

GRACE BEFORE MEALS

Bless us, O Lord, and these your gifts, which we are about to receive from your goodness, through Christ our Lord. Amen.

GRACE AFTER MEALS

We thank you, O Lord, for these gifts and for all the gifts we have received from your goodness, through Christ our Lord. Amen.

THE "MEMORARE"

Remember, O most gracious Virgin Mary, that never was it known that anyone who fled to your protection, implored your help or sought your intercession, was left unaided. Inspired with this confidence, I fly to you, O Virgin of virgins, my Mother; to you do I come, before you I stand, sinful and sorrowful. O Mother of the Word Incarnate, despise not my petitions, but in your mercy hear and answer me. Amen.

PRAYER TO THE HOLY SPIRIT

Come, O Holy Spirit, fill the hearts of Your faithful and kindle in them the fire of Your love.

> **V.** Send forth Your Spirit and they shall be created
> **R.** And You shall renew the face of the earth.

Let us pray:

O God, who has taught the hearts of the faithful by the light of the Holy Spirit, grant that in the same Spirit, we may be always truly wise and ever rejoice in His consolation. Through Christ our Lord. Amen.

SOUL OF CHRIST

(This is a prayer of Saint Ignatius Loyola)

Soul of Christ, sanctify me.
Body of Christ, save me.
Blood of Christ, inebriate me.
Water from the side of Christ,
    wash me.
Passion of Christ, strengthen me.
O good Jesus, hear me.
Within Your wounds, hide me.
Separated from You,
    let me never be.
From the malignant enemy,
    defend me.
At the hour of death, call me.
To come to You, bid me,
    that I may praise You
    in the company of Your saints,
    for all eternity. Amen.

MORNING PRAYER

Dear God, I thank you for watching over me during the night. Today I offer you my whole self: my every thought, word and act. Please keep me from harm. Bless my parents, my family and everyone I love.

EVENING PRAYER

Dear God, before I go to bed, please hear my last prayer. Thank you for all your help today. Forgive me any wrong I did. I am truly sorry. Keep in your care, my mother and father, and everyone I love. May the souls of the faithful departed, through the mercy of God, rest in peace. Amen.

A VISIT TO CHURCH

It is most pleasing to God when we make a visit to Church and speak to Jesus quietly and alone.

If we do this often, we shall grow very close to our Lord and his grace will be with us to guide our every moment.

In addition to our words and thoughts, the following prayers may be said:

ACT OF FAITH

O my God, I believe that you are one God in three Divine Persons: Father, Son and Holy Spirit. I believe that Your Divine Son became Man and died for our sins, and that He will come again to judge the living and the dead. I believe these and all the truths that the Catholic Church teaches, because You have revealed them, who can neither deceive nor be deceived. Amen.

ACT OF HOPE

O my God, relying on Your almighty power and infinite mercy and promises, I hope to obtain pardon of my sins, the help of Your grace and life everlasting, through the merits of Jesus Christ, my Lord and Redeemer. Amen.

ACT OF LOVE

O my God, I love you above all things with my whole heart and soul, because You are all good and worthy of all my love. I love my neighbor as myself for the love of You. I forgive all who have injured me and ask pardon of all whom I have injured. Amen.

THE BEATITUDES

1. Blessed are the poor in spirit: the reign of God is theirs.
2. Blessed are the sorrowing: they shall be consoled.
3. Blessed are the lowly: they shall inherit the land.
4. Blessed are they who hunger and thirst or holiness: they shall have their fill.
5. Blessed are they who show mercy: mercy shall be theirs.
6. Blessed are the single-hearted: for they shall see God.
7. Blessed are the peacemakers: they shall be called sons of God.
8. Blessed are those persecuted for holiness' sake: the reign of God is theirs.

THE CHIEF SPIRITUAL WORKS OF MERCY

To admonish the sinner.
To instruct the ignorant.
To counsel the doubtful.
To comfort the sorrowful.
To bear wrongs patiently.
To forgive all injuries.
To pray for the living and the dead.

THE CHIEF CORPORAL WORKS OF MERCY

To feed the hungry.
To give drink to the thirsty.
To clothe the naked.
To visit the imprisoned.
To shelter the homeless.
To visit the sick.
To bury the dead.

GUARDIAN ANGEL PRAYER

Angel of God
my Guardian dear
to whom God's love
commits me here.
Ever this day
be at my side
to light and guard
to rule and guide.
Amen.

MY OWN PRAYER FOR THIS SPECIAL DAY

_____

_____

_____

_____

_____

_____

_____

MY OWN PRAYER FOR MY FRIENDS

_____

_____

_____

_____

_____

_____

MY OWN PRAYER FOR MY FAMILY

_____

_____

_____

_____

_____

_____

_____

MY OWN PRAYER TO MY FAVORITE SAINT

_____

_____

_____

_____

_____

_____

_____

PERSONAL RECORD

Name _____
   born _____ in _____

Baptism
   Date _____
   Priest _____
   Parish _____
   Godfather _____
   Godmother _____

First Communion
   Date _____
   Priest _____
   Parish _____

Confirmation
   Date _____
   Bishop _____
   Parish _____
   Sponsor _____
   Confirmation name _____

FAMILY RECORD

Father_____
 born_____in_____

Mother_____
 born_____in_____

Brothers and Sisters_____
_____
_____

Father's Family
Grandfather_____
 born_____
Grandmother_____
 born_____

Mother's Family
Grandfather_____
 born_____
Grandmother_____
 born_____

PRAYER BEFORE A CRUCIFIX

Look down upon me, good and gentle Jesus, while I kneel and ask you to fill my heart with faith, hope, charity and true sorrow for my sins. Help me never to sin again.

I think of your five wounds with great love and pity as I repeat the words of your prophet, David, "They have pierced my hands and my feet; they have injured all my bones."

(Say one Our Father, Hail Mary, and Glory Be, for the Pope.)

"*I will be with you all Days,*

Even until the End of time."